Way Words
A Daily Itinerary for Lent

WAY WORDS
A DAILY ITINERARY FOR LENT

Copyright © 2011 by Abingdon Press

All rights reserved.

Library of Congress Cataloging-in-Publication Data

Indermark, John, 1950-
Way words : a daily itinerary for Lent / by John Indermark.
p. cm.
ISBN 978-1-4267-3065-8 (pbk. : alk. paper)
1. Lent--Meditations. 2. Bible--Meditations. I. Title.
BV85.I453 2011
242'.34--dc23
        2011025027

ISBN: 9781426730658

11 12 13 14 15 16 17 18 19 20—10 9 8 7 6 5 4 3 2 1

Manufactured in the United States of America

Way Words

A Daily Itinerary for Lent

by

John Indermark

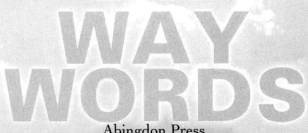

Abingdon Press
Nashville

WAY
WORDS

Dedication

This book is dedicated to the late
Helen Shovell Wilson,
Church Secretary and
Friend and Mother-in-law,
Whose faith and wisdom and love
has long guided me on the Way.

WAY
WORDS

Table of Contents

Acknowledgments

Like any other, *Way Words* is a book whose words owe to a multitude of sources—and whose coming to publication owes to even more. Ron Kidd at Abingdon Press became a valued and appreciated advocate for these words moving from proposed project to contracted work. From there, Jan Turrentine served as editor, giving guidance and direction in the initial stages of moving ideas into formed text—and then, honing and crafting that text through the editing process. Numerous others at Abingdon Press, including production editor Sheila Hewitt and designer Ken Strickland, have also contributed in matters of verification and further refining of the words you now see on these pages.

In June of 1974, I arrived in Portland, Oregon, to serve a year-long internship at Second (now Ainsworth) United Church of Christ. The church secretary was Helen Wilson, to whom this book is dedicated. Since my supervising pastor was himself an interim, only at church one day a week and Sundays, I worked on a daily basis most closely with Helen. She became a mentor in how ministry takes shape in and through the church office. She also became my friend. And in August of 1975, Helen became my mother-in-law. Until her death in February of 2010, Helen remained all three of those to me: mentor, friend, and mother-in-law. I truly miss her. But even more truly, I am grateful for all she was—and continues to be—in my journey on the Way.

Using This Book

One of the most ancient designations of the church as related in the *Book of Acts* was "The Way." Such a naming implies that journey and movement are inherent in Christian faith and discipleship. Lent brings such a season to Christian community in its journey directed toward Holy Week's passion and hope. *Way Words* offers a selection of daily readings from Ash Wednesday through Easter Sunday to serve, as the book's subtitle suggests, as a daily itinerary for your journey through the season of Lent.

The prophet Habakkuk speaks of being directed by God to "write a vision, and make it plain upon a tablet so that a runner can read it" (2:2). *Way Words* seeks to honor the spirit of that directive. Each daily reading in this Lenten itinerary explores a particular Way Word: a concise phrase or sentence that illuminates what it means to journey by faith. The word may be revealing of the God who bids us to this Way. The word may be revealing of our lives upon this Way. The word may be revealing of the world through which we travel, and for which we are to care, on this Way. Each daily Way Word comes from Scripture, except when noted, from the Common English Bible, for we are a people given identity and vocation from the biblical witness. The readings following each Way Word offer connection not only with the Lenten journey, but into the contemporary environs of present-day living.

The daily readings, except for the one for Ash Wednesday, are grouped into weeks. Each week's readings focus upon one of the following bedrock themes for the way of faith:

"Holy Foundations"	Assurances and promises made by or about God
"Godward Callings"	Calls evoking who we are to be as persons and communities

WAY WORDS

"Crucial Decisions" Choices facing those who would journey on faith's way

"Community Valuings" Qualities and characteristics of God-formed communities

"Faithful Practices" Practices of one's faith in daily life and relationships

"Enlarging Vistas" The broadening of our vision by the breadth and grace of God's vision

"Saving Mysteries" Remembrances of Table, Cross, Sabbath, and the Resurrected Way

As you journey through Lent with *Way Words*, please do only one reading per day (along with the accompanying prayer or spiritual exercise). Allow the reading some time to work in your mind and spirit throughout the day. Perhaps you might return to that reading in the evening, as you look back at the day now past. Where have this day's events and experiences taken you? How has this day's unfolding related to, or been shaped by, the Way Word for this day?

Prayerfully give the Holy Spirit and these words the freedom and opportunity to companion you through the Lenten journey—a journey that does not end so much as it begins anew with Easter's summons to journey on Christ's resurrecting Way.

John Indermark   *Eastertide 2011*

Ash Wednesday
Where Are You Going?

"Leave... for the land that I will show you."   *Genesis 12:1*

Where are you going?

Have you ever been asked that question by someone whose boundaries you may just have crossed, perhaps by someone who might be seeking a traveling companion?

Then again, have you ever gotten up the nerve to ask yourself that question when paths that once seemed certain suddenly grew desperately uncertain, when dead ends rose up or loose ends unraveled? *Just where am I going?*

Lent asks that question of individuals and communities of faith. It does so in the context of this season's traditional pilgrimage, beckoning our remembrance of the journey made by Jesus toward Jerusalem and Golgotha and beyond. But the Gospel's narrative is by no means the first story of a faithfully embodied response on the way one takes that lead to God.

On this Wednesday of ashes, when we may hear words of the dust from whence we have come and to whence we are going, another way is offered. It, too, is a dusty one, made by sandals plodding over rock and sand. Had the ones who so traveled been asked, "Where are you going?" the answer would likely have been disconcerting. *Well, really, we don't know. It's to a land we've been told that we'll be shown, but it's not in sight yet.* Father Abram and Mother Sarai make their way, not with GPS coordinates securely locked in to a clear destination, but with trust in the One who sets their faith-walk in motion:

Abram's and Sarai's way marks the opening of this Lenten journey. It is a way best made by those who are willing to trust, rather than requiring the end to be in sight or in hand before starting out. That might seem an odd way, an odd word, with which to start Lent. After all, we know what happens at the end.

Or do we? Do we know what will become of us by traveling Lent's way? Do we know ahead of time how this journey might transform or challenge us?

Where are you going this Lent? Are you on your way *to* a story you know by heart? Or are you on your way *in* a story meant to change your heart? That is, are you willing, with Abram and Sarai, to go to a land God will show you—if you are willing to leave behind what you know for the sake of Whom you trust?

Where are you going?

God, as I begin Lent's journey, help me trust your gracious companionship upon it. Wherever this way may lead, may I find—and be found in—you.

Week One
Holy Foundations

Thursday
"Everything came into being through the Word. . . . " **John 1:3**

One short day after you may have figuratively or literally donned the ashes of Lenten repentance, this strikingly different word is pronounced. Everything originates in the creative Word of God. Many words have flowed in an attempt to unpack the theological and philosophical nuances of the opening verses to John's gospel. Their oft-invoked celebration of the divine *logos*, that word we translate with a capitalized *Word* in English, seems more suited to reading by Christmas Eve candlelight than on the second day of Lent.

But on this day following the imposition of ashes, the word that John's Word imposes upon the way you would travel is a starkly simple one. Wherever you go today, whomever you meet, whatever situation you encounter: you are in the range, and likely in the midst, of God's creative purposes. This does not mean to suggest that every single detail of what unfolds in your life today will be God's irrevocable will. Nor does this presume that every single one with whom you share this journey acts in total obedience to God's purposes, including yourself. The random can occur. People can make bad choices. All those are givens. But do know that your journey today will never step beyond the boundaries, in space or relationship or circumstance, of something or someone that does not bear connection to God's creative workings. John's "everything came into being through the Word" assures the lingering potential of God acting creatively within or upon your life in this day.

In other words, today poses a *holy* moment ripe with possibilities for faithful response. Granted, that is a word entirely dependent upon faith. Not every situation facing you may be a pleasant one. Not every person encountered may be a source of unbridled joy. "Ripe with possibilities" might seem the farthest thing from your mind when you survey the lay of today's land. But as you consider what looms before you, remember to bring into its vision this affirmation from John's prologue. God's creative purposes, God's *Word* with a capital "W," form the foundation upon which you may stand and live as a person of faith. You are not on ground, nor in circumstances, that have been abandoned by God. The God who once fashioned everything through a Word, speaking Creation into being, may well speak again, for you and even through you, for the sake of new life.

Consider a difficult situation you face. What possibilities for God's creative purposes may be hidden within it? What might you do today to discern and act with trust in those purposes?

Friday
"It was supremely good." Genesis 1:31

One helpful method of exploring Scripture is to identify with a character in the passage at hand. How might you understand the parable of the prodigal son if you were to stand in the sandals of the elder son, or the younger, or the father of both? Or if the exercise involves selecting the character with whom you identify most closely, what might seeing yourself as the elder—or the younger, or the parent—reveal about who and where you are on faith's way?

As you look at the Way Word from Genesis 1:31, place yourself in its wider story. On the one hand, it is relatively easy to do. The whole verse has in view "everything [God] had made." Unless you consider yourself entirely self-made, you fit quite neatly into that verse's view. For some, however, the difficulty comes in accepting the assessment of all creation—or even one's own self—as "supremely good" in the eyes and judgment of God. But long before stories of "fall" and theologies of "utter depravity" enter the scene: God deems everything made by God, including you, as good.

"Goodness" is your starting point in creation. It is the God-endowed foundation upon which all else flows in the biblical narrative and, if the truth be told, in the narrative of your life. To affirm this truth does not deny what manages to scale over that goodness in the consequences of human sin or by powers ingrained in societal structures that corrupt the human spirit and despoil creation. To affirm this truth also does not give free reign to pride that claims goodness or perfection for self alone, while viewing others with disdain or subordination.

The foundation of goodness invests God's assessment and God's purposes into the very core of your being. Sin is not ultimately at the center of who you are; goodness is. You are not, in essence, an affront to God. You are part of the whole creation that God deemed good.

You are not served by a false humility that decries that you have nothing to offer to God or to others. You have goodness in you by the work of God's hand in your creation.

So blessed and deemed as good by God, you are free this day not only to be claimed by such goodness. You are free to live toward others and toward creation with such goodness.

Prayerfully reflect on what it means for you that the first word pronounced over your creation is not *sin* but *good*. How might you live out that truth in this day's choices and opportunities?

Saturday
"God...is compassionate and merciful"   Exodus 34:6

Did you know that Moses hailed from Missouri? I didn't either until I read Exodus 33. His accent gave him away. I don't mean "accent" as in an Ozark twang or a St. Louis pronunciation of *quarter* that rhymes with *water.* The Missouri accent came in Moses' pairing of a particular verb and pronoun in 33:13 and 18. Both contain the state motto of Missouri: *Show me.*

Moses wanted to be shown God's ways and God's glory. To set the context, Moses had just interceded on behalf of Israel in the wake of the golden calf fiasco. God had then informed Moses that he and the people could go on their merry way to the Promised Land but just not to expect God to go (33:3). Moses' pleas on behalf of the people turned aside that judgment. Armed with that success, Moses aimed higher. Now he would be shown who God is.

Be careful what you ask for, because you might just get it. Moses got his wish. But instead of a burst of holiness pyrotechnics that might dazzle momentarily, Moses got a more straightforward revealing of God's ways and glory. Accompanying the name first heard from a burning bush, Moses received the base-line revelation of God's identity: "compassionate and merciful."

If you want to be shown God, then be on the lookout for compassion and mercy.

Remember that on this journey you undertake in Lent. Compassion and mercy are at the heart of God's character revealed in the path that Jesus takes to Jerusalem. A path littered with forgiveness. A path strewn with embracings of lowly ones and lost ones. A path that leads to a hill where even executioners are interceded for. Compassion and mercy.

Remember this on the journey that is the whole of your life. If you want to be shown God, watch for compassion and mercy. It is a simple truth that often gets lost in the clatter of more strident appeals to God. God's hatred of this group or that, God's loathing of this sin or that—uncannily, that is the sin we usually profess in others rather than confess ourselves.

But remember: To a prophet who wanted to be shown God, God uses the adjectives *compassionate* and *merciful* to disclose not simply who God is but how God acts. That foundation remains the same for your faith. If you would be shown God, if you would *show* God, compassion and mercy persist as the ways and glory of God.

I confess you as compassionate and merciful, O God, for so you reveal yourself to me. May I live in ways compassionate and merciful, for so you would reveal yourself through me.

Sunday
"I will be kind to whomever I wish to be kind."   *Exodus 33:19*

Have you heard the expression of "putting God in a box"? It describes human attempts to predetermine what God can and cannot do. We might be more familiar with an older practice associated with such "boxing": idolatry. The real offense of fashioning gods is not the resulting image. It is, rather, the implication that we can manipulate handmade gods to do our bidding.

It is not coincidental that today's Way Word follows immediately upon Israel's crafting of a golden calf. The people sought to box God into an attractive package. Israel was weary of trust, and wanted to seize the initiative, to be in control, to dictate the terms, to fashion God in their own image. Such a malleable god would indeed seem golden.

God relented from plans to abandon this stiff-necked band. But relenting does not mean caving. To make sure that there were no mis-understandings about the impossibility of boxing God into a calf or anything else, God declared this foundational word to Israel—and to us: "I will be kind to whomever I wish to be kind." In other words, *don't box me in.*

That declaration might sound unnecessary. Don't we relish God's *kindness* (in Hebrew, this word carries the meaning of "grace" or "favor") in our lives? Are we not grateful for second and third and more chances for the likes of us and those like us? Possessive pronouns can be revealing. God's favor is fine when it embraces *us* and *ours*. But we might be tempted to narrow the boundaries of grace when it holds close those *others* we prefer to keep at arm's length. Toward those we view as outsiders, toward those we despise as enemies: We often long for God's judgment to be levied. Prayers offered in times of war or prior to elections sometimes tip our hand this direction. We would prefer to box in God's kindness to only those we deem deserving, which is to say, on our side.

21

In the face of human presumption about who does or does not merit divine favor, God asserts to Moses and all the rest of us God's exquisite freedom from our opinions and assumptions. "I will be kind to whomever I wish to be kind."

These words have import in Lent. In Jerusalem, political and religious authorities combined to crucify God's incarnate prerogative to act graciously. But come Easter morning, God will be God; and grace will have the final word. For Christ. For us. For life.

Consider someone you find terribly hard to be kind or gracious toward. How might God view that individual with the eyes of favor? How might God's view transform your own?

Monday
"I, the LORD, love justice." Isaiah 61:8

There are days when you might think that what God really loves is a good worship service. Think about all of the time and energy (and budget!) poured into special music and sermons, preparing the space with paraments and PowerPoint® presentations designed to catch the eye and touch the spirit. Then again, there are days when you might think that what God really loves is proper church structure. O, the passion poured and the churchmanship (or is it one-up-manship?) exercised in waging the battles of congregational autonomy or jurisdictional connectionalism, bishops or no bishops.

To paraphrase a thought from the TV show *Seinfeld*: not that there's anything wrong with those things. Who wants a bad worship experience? Who wants to disregard the truth that how the church gets structured has much to do with what we understand the church to be called to do. I get that.

But is all that what God *really* loves?

Some understand Isaiah 56–66 to have been addressed to the exiles who returned to Jerusalem after captivity in Babylon. They faced a daunting situation. The city had been leveled. The temple stood in ruins. With so much to do, it would have been natural to wonder about priorities. Well, if the foundation beneath all such rebuilding was to be on the basis of what God loves, Isaiah 61:8 laid down a very clear blueprint. "I, the LORD, love justice."

God loves justice. Isaiah 61:8 should have come as no surprise back then. A similar foundation of God's love of justice was laid back when Israel was poised at the edge of the Jordan, waiting to enter the Promised Land. Way back then, Deuteronomy 10:18 spoke of God as the One who executes justice for the vulnerable. A later verse offers the covenantal corollary for God's love of justice: "Justice, and only justice, you shall pursue" (Deuteronomy 16:20, NRSV). Even a player like David cannot help but sing, "The LORD loves justice" (Psalm 37:28).

Jesus understood that. His first public words in ministry, according to Luke, came by reading a passage from Isaiah about good news for the poor and liberation for the oppressed—and then by announcing, "Today, this scripture has been fulfilled" (Luke 4:21). Jesus' ministry is a lived expression of what God loves.

God loves justice.

Would a stranger be able to see that foundational gospel truth in your words and actions—and in those of your congregation? Do you love what God loves?

Think about a current situation where justice is imperiled. Given God's love of justice, what might God love for you to do? What will you do, for the love of God?

Tuesday
"I myself will be with you."   Matthew 28:20

Whom do you like most to have as company? How you answer might depend upon the occasion involved. The ideal companion at a dinner party might not be the ideal companion for a three-week road trip. But consider this slightly different question: Whom do you *need* most to have as company? Think of the ones you needed to have by your side, in your corner. As you grew and matured. As you sat in a doctor's office after hearing devastating news. As you resolved to stand up in your community for a cherished principle.

You and I need the presence of others in our lives, particularly in times of transition. To face significant matters buoyed by the renewal experienced in solitude is one thing. To face those same matters engulfed by the debilitation of loneliness is quite another.

Yet in those times of transition, and even in the midst of ordinary moments of reflection, we might find ourselves wondering about the limits imposed on such presence in our lives. Unless you live in very different conditions from those in which I do, you already know what it means to grieve the death of a friend or loved one. You already know what it means to wonder whether anything truly endures relationally on the other side of the grave—much less on this side, where estrangement or the simple reality of changing lives often moves even the closest to us out of our orb.

To disciples who likely wondered what was about to come of them when the one they followed prepared to leave, Jesus assured them of presence that would not fail. "I myself will be with you." God will be with you. Now. Tomorrow. For all time. Beyond time as we know it.

The assurance of God's presence sustained Jesus on the Jerusalem journey. The assurance of God's presence offers to sustain you on whatever journey lies ahead. Each of your days bears the hope and empowerment of "I myself will be with you."

Open yourself to God's presence, even and especially when it takes faith to do so. In your loneliness, you will not be alone. In the midst of swirling rushes of busyness, you will not be left to fend for yourself. In your grief, you will not be abandoned. In your living, in your dying, in that mystery that is beyond death: God will be with you.

Call to mind a situation you find difficult. Bring the promise of Christ into it: "I myself will be with you." Speak those words aloud into it. Allow God's presence to bear you through this time.

Wednesday
"God so loved the world."   John 3:16

Through this first week of Way Words offered for the Lenten journey and beyond, words of "holy foundations" have been the theme. The foundations affirmed have been varied: God's creative purposes woven into every one of your days; God's deeming all creation as good; God's character decisively revealed in compassion and mercy; God's freedom to be God; God's love for justice; and the enduring promise of God's presence.

To those foundations comes this concluding Way Word. It is the word binding together all these other foundations, revealing both their source and goal. "God so loved the world."

The familiarity of those words may work against their stunning declaration: God loves the world. Think about that. Think about that as you view the local or national or international news tonight. The unrest, the conflicts, the all-too-prevalent accounts of inhumane actions and invective words aimed against those deemed as enemies or opposition—or sometimes the utterly random violence that has no target outside of anything that gets in its way. You might think, with a host of others, that this world is headed to hell in a handbasket. Which is to say, you might have thought that God had given up on this world.

But God did not. And God does not. For God so loves the world.

That is not to say that God loves all that happens in this world, of which the paragraph above touches only on the tip of the iceberg. God is not blind or deaf. But neither is God a quitter. God may rage against such inhumanity, as the prophets of Israel make abundantly clear. And we should rage as well. But God does not give up on the world. God sends *into* the world, as John 3:16 goes on to affirm, the gift of the Beloved.

"God so loved the world." That is the foundation for the story of Lent. It was so in the life of Jesus. For in spite of detractors and betrayers and executioners: God's love for the world set the direction and resolve for Jesus' journey. That is also the foundation for your life in this season and all seasons. Even when the world seems inhospitable to its possibility, God's love for the world intends to set the direction and resolve for your life as a disciple of Jesus. For you and I are to live as signs and embodiments of that love of God.

Help me, O God, to find in your love for the world, a way for me to be an instrument of that love. Not because I must, but because I am loved. By you. In Jesus Christ. Amen.

Week Two
Godward Callings

Thursday
"God created humanity in God's own image." *Genesis 1:27*

What is on your to-do list for today? A phone call you need to make? A long-overdue visit to a friend or family member? What else might today hold in store for you? After all, to-do lists have a way of expanding as the day unfolds. When those unanticipated responsibilities or unexpected situations arise, just what are you supposed to do?

Today's Way Word, from Genesis, provides one standing order for this day's to-do list. You are to be an image of God in the world. What you do in and with your relationships and choices is to "image" something of who God is and what God values in life.

The significance of this calling to be an image of God is underscored in another tradition about images and God. The King James Version of Exodus 20:4 forbids the fashioning of any "graven images." Nothing fashioned by human hands can be or do what God has created you for. Revealing God is the response-ability of humankind. It is your responsibility.

Scholars link this functional understanding of "image of God" with the practice of ancient rulers who set up statues (images) of themselves across their dominion, conveying their presence and power even when they were not physically present. While not perfect, the analogy affirms that the human calling to be the "image of God" involves conveying God's presence and purposes in the world.

The Lenten narrative of Jesus' journey toward Jerusalem provides a model for what such "imaging" involves. For example, Jesus images the grace of God in his revealings of the wide embrace of God's love. Sometimes he does this in words, as in the parable of the prodigal son or in his forgiving of those who crucified him. Sometimes he does this in actions, as in sharing the Last Supper with the one who betrayed him or in assuring a dying thief of a place in Jesus' kingdom. For those with ears to hear and eyes to see, Jesus' words and actions serve as an image of God.

Neither of us is Jesus. But you and I are created in—and created to be—the image of God. You and I are called to reveal something of God in what we do and say and value.

So put this at the top of your to-do list for today, and let it permeate everything you do. Be an image of God.

Reflect on your life yesterday. Where and how did you reveal something of God? Look ahead at the day before you. How might you be an image of God in its opportunities and responsibilities?

Friday
"Get going. I'm sending you." Exodus 3:10

When was the last time someone sent you somewhere? Was it a moment marked by excitement or dread? Were you delighted to be chosen, or were you scrambling to suggest another to go instead of you?

God told Moses: "Get going. I'm sending you." It is worth noting that the words leading up to this explain how the Israelites' cries of injustice under Pharaoh reached God. And how God, in turn, had seen how much the Egyptians had oppressed the people. So you might have thought that God would have told Moses: "I'm on my way!"

Actually, that is what God said. It's just that God would be on the way by way of what surely was a somewhat surprised Moses, who set out that day intending to simply tend sheep. That surprise may be evident in Moses' initial response: "Who am I to go?" (Exodus 3:11). Being sent can be unnerving, then and now.

This story of being sent by God on a mission repeats itself. It certainly does so in the life and ministry and passion of Jesus. "For God so loved the world that...." What comes next? God *sent*. The narrative that the season of Lent engages is all about the ways in which that sending and its love get embodied. God's *sending* results in Jesus' *coming*.

It is a story that still repeats itself. When cries for help spiral toward God, when God's love seeks renewed witness and embodiment, guess what? "Get going. I'm sending *you*." No longer is the "you" in that quotation the long-ago figure of Moses sent to the Israelites in captivity. "I'm sending you" intones the ongoing habit of God to call on individuals and communities in every age to be instruments of God's working and embodiments of God's love. And if you should respond, as Moses before you, with "Who am I to go?" The answer is: You are the one God chooses. You are the one God loves.

"I'm sending you." Be assured that God is speaking in present tense to none other than you. You are the one God calls to rise and be on

your way—that is, on God's way—today. You are the one God now sends. Where and with whom will you be today? What might be a word or an act that might bear the presence or love of God in that moment?

"Get going. I'm sending you."

God, be with me in this day. Help me discern opportunities for being an instrument of your presence or love. Lead me by your Spirit where and to whom you would send me.

Saturday
"Hate evil, love good, and establish justice at the city gate." Amos 5:15

There are evils that should be hated: abusing a child, embezzling what someone has put aside or been promised for retirement, taking pleasure in inflicting pain.

There are goods that should be loved: respecting the good God fashioned in another, doing what is just for and with those in need of justice, treating creation as the work of God's hands.

What do you hate? What do you love? And what is the link between them?

Let me suggest one possibility: passion. Passion figures prominently in the season of Lent. Its Greek root means "to suffer." Long before Mel Gibson chose it for a movie title, *the passion of the Christ* referred to Jesus' sufferings. Over time, the original meaning of *passion* has been expanded by contemporary associations with *passionate*. To be passionate for something or someone is to have intense feelings toward it or him or her. And not feelings alone. For *passionate* also suggests a willingness to have those passions trigger actions.

Some religious impulses would tamp down the fires of passion and not simply those related to sexual impulses. Moderation in all things would be the byword of that approach. Don't go overboard one way or another. Keep to the middle. Don't rock the boat. We have all kinds of expressions for that. There is some wisdom there, but there is also danger. Revelation 3:15-16 takes aim at that danger in one early church community. "You are neither cold nor hot. So ... I'm about to spit you out." Lukewarm is not a spiritual safety zone.

Why? Times come when moderation doesn't cut it. Amos understood that. You cannot be "moderately" against evil. You cannot be "moderately" for good. Passion is not necessarily a sign of zealotry. In the face of evil or good, passion may be the mark of faithfulness.

Consider Jesus when he confronts the moneychangers and animal salesmen. Overturning tables of business people is not moderate. It is passionate. It is passionate hatred of seeing a holy place made into a marketplace. It is passionate love for the sanctity of his Father's house.

The passion of the Christ is not only what happens in betrayal and trial and crucifixion when suffering does come. The passion of the Christ is also what Jesus does throughout his ministry in hatred of evil and love of good.

What do you hate? What do you love? And how do they relate to the passion of Christ?

Write a journal entry that explores what you are passionate about in life. What hatreds or loves are involved? In what ways do you express your passion? Where is God in those passions?

Sunday
"Follow me, ... and I'll show you how to fish for people." **Mark 1:17**

In my first parish, I decided to pursue fly-fishing. I bought the equipment. I read the books. I flailed away on the water. I even caught a few fish. The decisive turn did not come, however, until I started fishing with my friend Lee. I don't remember who found out first about the other's interest in fly-fishing. But the connection was made. Lee took me under his wing—or should I say, out with our waders and float tubes. Lee invited me to follow him—to Bayley and McDowell Lakes, to Sullivan Creek and the Pend Oreille River—and showed me how to fly-fish.

"Follow me." Jesus bids these fishers by Galilee's sea to journey with him. Sometimes the church puts the cart before the horse when it comes to discipleship. Biblical scholars and theologians try to parse the implications of what it means to follow Jesus. Preachers proclaim three-point summaries or engage in Lenten explorations on the hallmarks of discipleship. But let's be clear. In the text, "follow me" begins with placing one foot after the other on the path taken by Jesus. It is only by setting out on this particular journey that the disciples come to learn—by experience—what following Jesus means.

"I'll show you how to. . . ." To fishers, Jesus framed the invitation to follow on the basis of familiar experience given a new twist. "How to fish" they already knew. "For people" was the new challenge, whose learning would come only by experiencing Jesus at work. Imagine Jesus speaking to you now: "I'll show you how to. . . ." What words would frame that invitation to you? As with fishers of old, what experience might you bring that Christ would tweak with the new challenge that comes in learning—by experience—what following Jesus means?

"Follow me, . . . and I'll show you how to. . . ." A word of warning: Lee could have just told me what he does when and where he fishes and why he does it. But to learn, I needed to follow him into the water.

Jesus' invitation is not exhausted by reading devotional books or thinking pious thoughts. Jesus bids you to put one foot after the other in his footsteps today. Where and among whom might that be? The stories of Scripture may provide the clues. But discipleship unfolds on the way we choose to take one step at a time.

Who are your mentors in Christian faith and discipleship? What is it that you have learned from them, and how? If possible, let them know what they have done for you.

Monday
"Whoever serves me must follow me." John 12:26

You might have thought that the verse should read: Whoever *follows* me must *serve* me. Then again, Jesus clarifies elsewhere that he "didn't come to be served but rather to serve" (Mark 10:45). So if following Jesus is the prerequisite for serving Jesus, and not the other way around, where exactly will following Jesus lead you in preparation for your Christ-like serving of others?

Right into the ground.

The verses immediately prior to John 12:26 relate how pilgrims in Jerusalem for the Passover went to Philip with a request: "Sir, we want to see Jesus" (John 12:21). When this request was passed on to Jesus, he responded in two ways: Jesus first announced that the time of his glorification had come. And then, Jesus told the single-verse parable of the grain of wheat. That is the story where a single grain of wheat remains just that unless it is buried in the ground. Only then, from within the ground, does new life and harvest spring. After adding his own interpretation to the parable, Jesus declared today's word that those who would serve him must follow him.

Right into the ground.

John's gospel is famous for misunderstandings based on literal interpretations. Nicodemus couldn't imagine getting back into his mother's womb to be born again. Opponents disputed how someone who called himself "the bread of life" could give his flesh to eat. So do not think that the parable's implication that following Jesus takes you "right into the ground" requires a shovel or a backhoe. What following does require, in that parable and the approaching narrative of Jesus' passion, is trust of God in the most radical of ways. The trust that God can bring life out of death. The trust that then *en-trusts* life—and death—into the hands of God.

So what has following Jesus into the ground of trust to do with serving him? The fruits of your service may not always, or even often, be self-evident. Seeds planted in compassion, in justice, in mercy, in forgiveness may take time to sprout—time longer than your presence in that situation or relationship, perhaps time longer than your lifespan. To serve Jesus trusts God that what you do and say and who you are have worth and value and impact beyond your ability to see what results.

If you would risk serving Jesus, follow him into the ground, where trust of God is all.

In what ways do you see your service grounded in trust of God? How might your service be deepened or expanded by more intentional linkage of it with such trust?

Tuesday
"I must stay in your home today."   Luke 19:5

Getting your home ready for visits can be such a chore. Dusting corners you've ignored for some time. Putting things away that you'd prefer your company not see, lest you or they be embarrassed.

So imagine what you might be doing today to get your home ready for a visit from Jesus.

In the town of Jericho, Jesus reverses the usual order of hospitality and invites himself in to the home of Zacchaeus. The little guy who climbed up a tree to catch a glimpse of the celebrity rabbi now hears himself called out by Jesus. "I must stay in your home today." And my, oh my, are there ever corners to be dusted and things to be put away! A neighborhood reputation for being a sinner. A hoard of wealth from an overzealous pursuit of his vocation that, by implication of his later words to Jesus, involved fraud and cheating. Into that home Jesus invites himself. You might even say that Jesus barges in: "I *must* stay in your home."

That is when the housecleaning begins. To one who apparently has passed much of his life attempting to accumulate all that he can, Zacchaeus dusts out the corners by declaring half of his possessions will now be given into the possession of the poor. Zacchaeus puts away the embarrassing trail of fraud, not by hiding it out of Jesus' sight — sight good enough, you will recall, to spot this wee little man up in a tree. No, Zacchaeus puts it away by bringing it into broad daylight in his vow to restore fourfold what he has cheated anyone out of. Zacchaeus sets quite a table for this rabbi who invites himself in — and who now declares, running a spiritual white glove over the cleaning Zacchaeus has done, "Today, salvation has come to this household."

So tell me, friend, did salvation come when Jesus walked in the door, or when Zacchaeus made ready his home?

Good storyteller that he is, Luke leaves you to ponder that question. Because good evangelist that he is, Luke presents you with the same words aimed at Zacchaeus: "I must stay in your home today."

What corners of your life need sweeping? What needs to be put away, not as in hidden but as in eliminated so that you may offer hospitality to the One whose grace would barge in to your life today?

Prayerfully consider what God would find welcoming in your life, and what you value or pursue that might not be hospitable to God's presence in your life. What will you do about the latter?

Wednesday
"We are ambassadors who represent Christ." 2 Corinthians 5:20

Ambassadors for Christ, by Dr. Anthony Bash, explores New Testament passages related to ambassadors. He does so in light of the functions of ambassadors in the eastern Roman Empire. The roles Bash lifts up include carrying out an appointed task that communicates the words and/or promotes the interests of someone else. "Someone else" typically was the Empire, for whom the ambassador acted as its representative diplomat. However, an "ambassador" could also represent a city or province or even an individual.

"We are ambassadors who represent Christ." So Paul imparted this calling to the Corinthian Christians. The functions of that office would have been familiar to them from their culture. Corinth was the capital of the Roman province of Achaia. Ambassadors to and from their province would have been nothing out of the ordinary. It stands to reason that, from their familiarity with that office, they would have likely heard Paul's words in the roles ambassadors played in those days. Ambassadors who represented Christ would be charged with communicating the words and promoting the interests of Christ to the wider culture in which they lived or to which they were sent.

Paul's calling to those long ago Corinthians remains in effect today. Ambassadors who communicate the words and promote the interests of Christ are still needed here and now. The "diplomatic corps" of this calling now, as then, is not limited to a few elite singled out for unique appointment. This calling extends to the whole community. In doing so, it extends to you. You are an ambassador who represents Christ.

How do you represent Christ in the world?

This day before you will bring opportunities and challenges to speak words that convey the spirit of Christ, perhaps in stark contrast to other words spewed in the spirit of reprisal or fear or indifference.

Christ would be represented in words marked by grace. Words marked by truth. Words marked by love. As Christ's ambassador, speak those words on Christ's behalf.

This day will also bring you opportunities and challenges to promote the interests of Christ, perhaps in stark contrast to other interests vying for allegiance. How might you represent Christ's interests? By seeking and doing justice. By practicing compassion. By extending the gift and offer of God's forgiveness. By engaging in the ministry of reconciliation. As Christ's ambassador, promote those interests on Christ's behalf.

For you are an ambassador who represents Christ.

Holy God, revealed to us in Jesus, what are your words that wait on my tongue to speak? What are your interests that you would have me do? How would you have me represent you in this day?

Week Three
Crucial Decisions

Thursday
"Choose today whom you will serve."   *Joshua 24:15*

In 1979, Bob Dylan recorded *Slow Train Coming,* an album that reflected his recent conversion to Christianity. Among its songs, "Gotta Serve Somebody" brings this message: No matter who you are or what your position in life, you end up serving somebody. You have to choose.

It is not a new insight.

Joshua gathered the tribes of Israel at Shechem. The land once promised was now largely in their possession. Having reviewed the history of their deliverance from the vantage point of God's perspective ("I took Abraham your ancestor.... I brought your ancestors out of Egypt.... I gave you land"), Joshua shifted to the matter of whom the tribes will now serve. Will it be the gods of Abraham's ancestors? Will it be the gods of the Egyptians? Will it be the gods of the peoples whose land Israel now possessed? Will it be the God whose saving actions are at the heart of the story just recounted by Joshua?

Such a choice might seem antiquated today. Modernity scoffs at beliefs in multiple deities associated with particular places or peoples. Enlightened thinkers and believers have moved past such superstitions.

But listen carefully to the choice posed by Joshua. Its focus is not on doctrinal matters: "What do you believe?" Its focus is on lived

allegiance: "Whom you will serve?" When it comes to allegiance and service, there is no shortage of gods in the modern world vying for your loyalty. You might no longer call them "gods"; but if something lays ultimate claim on your allegiance, be it nationalism or political philosophy or economic theory, how does that differ from the choices of deity that Joshua puts before Israel? What clamors for your service and loyalty?

Joshua's choices in gods raise intriguing possibilities for modern counterparts. *The gods of Abraham's ancestors.* Nostalgia can be a potent idol in faith. *The gods of the Egyptians.* Power that dominates can be an attractive alternative to power humbly exercised in servanthood. *The gods of the Amorites in whose land you live.* "Everybody around here is doing it" can be a seductive claim when discipleship beckons a costlier integrity to one's own peculiar values and commitments.

"Choose this day whom you will serve." Joshua and Bob Dylan agree that a choice must be made. So does Jesus: "No one can serve two masters" (Matthew 6:24).

Whom will you serve?

Whom will you serve? Hold Joshua's question before you this day. In the situations you enter, into the decisions before you, how might your choices reveal whom and what you actually serve in life?

Friday
"Jonah got up—to flee to Tarshish from the LORD!" Jonah 1:3

If ever a prophet needed a public relations firm to restore a besmirched reputation, Jonah surely fits that bill. Generations of preachers, including me, have verbally scourged this poor fellow. He is the one who headed west when God said: *Go east, young man.* He is the one who pronounced God's judgment against hated Nineveh, only to have God do a 180-degree turn. He is the one who would rather die than live with a spared Nineveh. "Don't be a Jonah" has become the church's standard advice.

But today I say to you: Give Jonah his due. It might seem that Jonah fled out of hatred for the Ninevites. After all, this sworn enemy of Jonah's people would have been held by Israel and Judah in similar distain as members of al-Qaeda would be at Ground Zero in New York.

Except, hatred is not the real reason Jonah heads west instead of east. The cause for his flight was not even that Jonah misunderstands God. Quite the opposite. Jonah flees, as chapter 4 reveals, because Jonah knows God all too well. "This is why I fled.... I know that you are a merciful and compassionate God" (4:2). Give Jonah credit: He takes God seriously.

In this odd counter-intuitive way, Jonah witnesses to the decision that Christian faith inevitably poses to you and to all. That would be the decision of discipleship: the decision to follow Jesus, to align yourself with the ways of God. In other words, the decision to take God seriously in your life. Jonah serves as a reminder that discipleship's chief difficulty may come not so much in *not* getting what God is about, but getting it all too well. Recall that Peter rebukes Jesus for speaking of a messiah who suffers and dies. Peter's rebuke arises not out of misunderstanding, but out of understanding Jesus all too well and taking him seriously.

Jonah decides to head west because he knows God all too well and takes God seriously.

Where does your knowing God all too well and taking God seriously lead you? When you hear Jesus command love of enemy, do you set out in flight for Tarshish or in mission to Nineveh? When you encounter Jesus forgiving those who crucify, which direction do you head?

Either direction may be chosen when you take God seriously. Which direction will you decide to take today?

Help me, O God, to take you as seriously as Jonah did. And then help me not to *flee from* but to *follow* on the path you would have me choose as your disciple.

Saturday
"Speak. Your servant is listening."   1 Samuel 3:10

An earlier verse in 1 Samuel 3 relates the crisis that sets the context for today's Way Word. "The LORD's word was rare at that time" (verse 1).

You and I live in a time when there is no scarcity of words. The printed word may be struggling financially, but most cable or satellite TV packages will buy you access to hundreds of channels inundating you with words 24/7. If you find nothing of interest on any of those channels (not an infrequent occasion in my household), power up the Internet and surf to your heart's desire. You will be swamped with words, many unedited and unchecked for veracity.

Therein lies the underlying dilemma in 1 Samuel 3. Words may not be rare in our time, but can they be trusted? On those ad-infinitum-to-the-point-of-ad-nauseum numbers of channels and websites, myriad voices claim the mantle of "Thus says the Lord." But can they all be equally trusted?

The decision of whom you listen to is really a matter of whom you trust. Young Samuel is directed by his elder mentor, Eli, to respond to the voice calling in the night, "Speak. Your servant is listening." Eli does so because he realizes that the voice is God's. Is Samuel himself so convinced? The narrative does not say. But Samuel trusts Eli enough to take him at his word. He listens to Eli. In doing so, he opens himself to listening to the voice of God.

Whom do you listen to, whom do you trust when it comes to directing your listening to God's addressing of your life? It is a decision you have to make, unless you want to trust that every voice claiming God's authority on TV and the Internet (not to mention all the pulpits in this land!) is justified in doing so. The choices of whom you trust to listen to will affect what you come to believe. For example, the consequences of deciding to listen with trust to Rachel Maddow or Rush

Limbaugh will shape your political views. It is the same with discerning the Word God seeks to speak amidst all of the talking heads and Internet scripts. Whom do you trust?

Maybe the Word of God is as rare in our time as in Samuel's. If so, that makes your decision of whom you will listen to all the more critical.

"Speak. Your servant is listening."

Make a list of people you listen to: "listening to" as in trusting their word. Who are those people when it comes to faith? In what ways has listening to them helped you to listen to and for God?

Sunday
"People won't live only by bread." Matthew 4:4

In the wilderness, hungry himself, Jesus does not discount the necessity of bread. To say that people won't live "only by bread" does not mean that people can live without bread. It has been estimated that 925 million people in 2010 suffered from hunger and malnutrition. The provision of food to hungry ones remains a compelling mandate for Christian compassion and justice.

Jesus simply emphasizes that bread *alone* does not satisfy the whole of life's needs. Back in the days of my youth, *bread* was a synonym for money. In the context of this verse, you could further expand its meaning to "stuff" and still be on target for Jesus' message. *People won't live only by stuff, but by* _____. And you fill in the blank. What do people strive for to find meaning, to achieve security, to secure power? You and I construct our lives around our answers to that. Consider how Jesus fills in that blank for himself in the second half of this verse: "every word spoken by God."

Keep in mind the context of this Way Word. Jesus is in a lonely place. He is hungry. The tempter comes along with an easy solution to it all. "Command these stones to become bread" (verse 3). Take a shortcut. Cut a corner. Follow the path of least resistance.

But the path Jesus has come to follow, which Lent bids you to come and see and then follow yourself, is not about ease or shortcuts. It is about faithfulness. It is about deciding what truly constitutes life for us.

People won't live only by bread. One estimate for the 2010 world population is 6.8 billion. That means, in tandem with the earlier statistic about world hunger, that billions of people do not suffer hunger for lack of bread. Among them, millions enjoy extraordinary affluence. But that does not mean that such folks do not hunger. That does not mean that you do not hunger. For meaning. For purpose. For connection

to something greater than what you can eat or bank or show on an insurance inventory.

All manner of choices are made in terms of what people seek beyond bread to bring life. In the wilderness, even in the experience of hunger, Jesus chose faithfulness to God's words and purposes. It would be a choice repeated time and again on his journey to Jerusalem.

What do you choose beyond bread to bring life?

Feed me, O God, with that which my life needs at this moment. Nourish me, Holy Spirit, with what will sustain me in the long run. Nurture me, Christ, in your faithfulness upon the way.

Monday
"You are lacking one thing." Mark 10:21

Most days, I'd be happy to have someone tell me that I was lacking in only one thing. What with seeking to be a good husband and father, trying to write words that others will find of interest and significance, attempting to keep up with the yard work, and striving to contribute in positive ways to church and community and nation: You mean I'm falling behind on only *one* thing?

You would think *that* would be good news to anyone! Unless the one thing singled out is the one thing that you or I would prefer to keep to ourselves. Unchallenged. Undisturbed. Intact.

That would seem to be the rub for the individual whom Jesus addresses with today's Way Word. Make no mistake; this individual presents an impressive resume. His lifetime of commandment-keeping suggests that he is one who, when he sets his mind on doing something, can and will achieve it. There is nothing in the text that would indicate that he is disingenuous in asking Jesus, "What must I do to obtain eternal life?" (verse 17).

Mark notes that Jesus loved him. Is the love generated by the question that is asked? Is the love generated by this individual's keeping of all of the commandments since his childhood? Mark does not say. But in Mark's construction, Jesus' love sets the context for Jesus' words: "You are lacking one thing." The prescription for dealing with that lack comes in four subsequent verbs: *Go. Sell. Give. Follow.*

The individual follows the first dictate. He goes. But dismay and sadness mark that departure, and the story ends with the other three verbs left undone. Why? "Because he had many possessions."

Jesus touches a raw nerve here. Possessions can possess you. But even more fundamentally than the hazard posed by wealth, amply spelled out in the following verses, "you are lacking one thing" points

to a more universal concern for discipleship. Namely, what would stand between you and your following of Christ? What would block your ability to entrust yourself to God wholly and without reservation?

Imagine yourself in the place of this individual in Mark. Jesus stands before you. He looks upon you with love. Out of that love, he says: "You are lacking one thing." What would be that one thing for you? What would be its equivalent of "Go, sell, give, follow"?

Jesus does look upon you with love. What will you choose to do?

Write a journal entry that reflects on that imagined encounter with Jesus at the end of today's reading. What is it that you can, and will, do today to address that "lack"?

Tuesday
"Take up [your] cross daily." Luke 9:23

I have sometimes heard someone speak of having to "bear a cross." In those hearings, the "cross" has consisted of an imposed burden thrust upon someone without choice. Sometimes the burden has been substantial. Chronic illness. The grief generated by a loved one's sudden death. Sometimes "bearing a cross" has been trivialized in reference to some minor inconvenience or inconsequential development.

In any such case, the bearing or taking up of one's cross in those terms misses the key dynamic of Jesus' words. Taking up one's cross is a voluntary act. It results from and speaks of the intentional decision to risk following God. The Gospels' narrative of Jesus' journey to and sojourn in Jerusalem reveals the risk Jesus entailed by trusting God in the face of political and religious institutions intolerant of higher allegiances than those they claimed for their own authority. It still is risky to not yield the trust and allegiance owed to God alone that contemporary institutions would beckon or coerce from us. Such a decision to follow God is not a burden imposed upon us. It is a choice Christ invites us to joyfully and freely make. *Taking up your cross* is an act of radical trust in God, come what may.

Matthew, Mark, and Luke all narrate this account of Jesus bidding the disciples and the crowd to take up their cross. But Luke alone adds one critical word to this call: *daily*. "Take up your cross" has often been associated with a singular decisive moment of turning to Jesus. I have known folks who told me the day and time and location of their decision to take up the cross and follow Jesus. I understand that.

But please do not miss what Luke reports as Jesus' words. The decision to take up your cross is not a once-and-for-all, never-to-be-repeated phenomenon. You and I are to take up the cross daily. In every crossroads you face about which path you will take, the invitation is

there. Take up your cross daily. In every opportunity you encounter to place your ultimate trust in God or something (or
someone) less, the call is there. Take up your cross daily.

Your cross is not a burden over which you have no
choice. Your cross is your daily commitment to follow the
path of love and servanthood traveled by Jesus.

Take up your cross, not because you must, but because
you may.

Look at the choices you face in this and coming days. What
might "take up your cross" mean in their light? How might
your cross not be an imposed burden, but a choice borne of
trust in God?

Wednesday
"I'm standing at the door and knocking."   Revelation 3:20

Do you consider yourself a hospitable person? That is, if someone comes knocking at your front door (or ringing the doorbell), would you be inclined to at least see who it is? And what would determine your decision to open the door or not?

Today's Way Word comes from a portion of Revelation that addresses the early Christian community at Laodicea. Several major trade and travel routes passed through the city, so it would have been a place where hospitality was not only valued but expected. A stranger should not be left outside, knocking on a door or gate, without answer. One could never be sure of who might be turned away or what opportunity might be lost if the knock went unanswered.

In the context of Revelation 3, this is no stranger or traveling trader awaiting someone within the community of Laodicea to open the door. This is the "faithful and true witness" (verse 14). This is Christ. The artist Warner Sallman portrayed this scene in a painting you may be familiar with. If not, you can easily see it online by entering the artist's name and the painting's title, "Christ at Heart's Door" in a search engine. It has been noted that in the image, there is no outside knob or latch to gain entry. The door can be opened only from the inside.

That detail is not represented in Revelation's verse. Yet, the painting is faithful to the verse's spirit. And it is faithful to the choice which underlies Revelation's challenge of Laodicea and discipleship's call to you. Christ may come calling in any number of ways and times. The question is: Will you prove hospitable to Christ's presence and leading? Will you choose to open the door?

The choice comes with complications or opportunities, depending upon your point of view. Opening the door to Christ's presence and leading will change you. It will change you because Christ's love seeks embodiment in your life. It will change you because the company Christ keeps in the least and lowly (Matthew 25:40) seeks your practices of hospitality and justice toward and with such ones.

Will those changes be complications or opportunities for you? Only you can say. Even as only you can open the door to the One who comes calling with such grace in hand with which to receive you—and to commission you to live graciously.

What will you decide when Christ comes knocking today?

I open my heart and mind; I open my will and spirit; I open my fears and hopes; I open my doubt and faith. To you, O God, I open the whole of myself. Open to me your opportunities for this day.

Week Four
Community Valuings

"Seeing your face is like seeing God's face." **Genesis 33:10**

If you were asked to draw a picture of God, what image(s) would you choose? An old man with a long beard? An exploding supernova? A child molding clay? A woman giving birth?

A researcher named Helmut Hanisch did a study in 1992 of pictures German children and youth had drawn of God. More than half of those who grew up in a religious environment pictured God in human form. Six percent of those participants portrayed God simply as a face.

Jacob had been running away from Esau for much of his life. He originally fled in fear of Esau's retaliation for Jacob's deceit in stealing the blessing their father had intended for Esau. Jacob now wants to come home. In spite of the lingering fear of his brother's retaliation, he presses on. When the reunion finally happens, Jacob's fears are met with Esau's *grace*. In the experience of such grace, Jacob confesses that his brother's face is like unto the face of God.

Why?

Is it because a face remembered only in fear conveys the look of acceptance and forgiveness? Is it because Esau is the one who runs to meet and embrace and kiss his long estranged brother before Jacob speaks a word? The writer of Genesis was wise to leave the matter unclear. Doing so leaves open the possibility for you to discern what of God might be seen in Esau's face. And that, in turn, opens for you the possibility of what it is you might see of God in a face you encounter today.

That is, after all, at the heart of Jesus' coming to us. God has put a face on love. That is, after all, at the heart of the church's calling to be the body of Christ: to put a face on that same love on Christ's behalf.

That the children in Hanisch's study often drew God in human form accentuates a foundational truth in Christian faith. Human form and human relationship are where God must be found if God is to be found at all. Jacob sees something of the face of God in Esau.

In whose face do you catch a glimmer of God's love and grace? And who might rely today on your face to reveal something to them of the love and grace of God?

Draw a picture of God. Afterward, offer a prayer that reflects whatever that picture represents for you.

Friday
"God heard their cry of grief, and God remembered his covenant."
Exodus 2:24

Eighteenth-century deism sought to extract God from the messy affairs of human history. Deism portrayed God as a clockmaker who intricately fashioned the "movement" that is creation, then set the timepiece to tick away on its own. A similar image depicted God as Architect of All, who then withdraws so that humanity can be guided by its God-given gift of reason. But where does hope lie when men and women, and the institutional powers they create, act unreasonably? Unjustly? Without compassion? What happens when the appeals of reason fall on ears that are indifferent if not hostile to those appeals?

The descendants of Israel suffered in Egypt under such oppressive power. Out of pain and fatigue, the people cried out. The text does not even say that they cried out to God. It simply says, "They cried out" (Exodus 2:23). If deism is true, if God is a card-carrying non-interventionist, the Hebrews captive in Egypt's bondage are out of luck. They are speaking into a void.

But they are not. "God heard their cry ... and God remembered" (verse 24). From this act of hearing and remembrance comes intervention celebrated by Israel as deliverance. God valued relationship and human community to the extent that God was willing to engage in human and social affairs for the sake of transformation. Exodus is not the story of an aloof clockmaker or distant architect. Exodus is the story of a redeemer who obtains freedom for a people oppressed.

Do you believe that story? Do you believe that God hears and remembers—and intervenes?

That is the invitation—and that is the scandal, for some—of today's Way Word for discipleship. Contemporary versions of deism would set aside "antiquated" views of prayer and liturgy that seek God's intervention as a logical impossibility.

But at what cost? Do worship and prayer then ultimately reduce to generating good thoughts about ourselves and how we can better our world, appending the name of God or Christ to our words so that we keep some semblance of tradition? Or do prayer and worship seek encounter with One who is more than simply present to our celebrations of life and community, or to our grievings of their brokenness or failures? Do prayer and worship seek the God who may intervene in response to cries for and by vulnerable ones?

When you pray today, do you believe that God hears and might intervene? If not, why do you pray?

Make a list of the things and the ones you pray for today. Why are these things and these ones of value to you? to God? What are you seeking God to hear? to remember? to do?

Saturday
"I will put my spirit within you, and you shall live."
Ezekiel 37:14 (NRSV)

It may be that this word does not strike you as terribly unusual. The church regularly, or at least on the day of Pentecost, alludes to God's bestowing of Spirit to bring life. There is no shock value in this Way Word, in and of itself.

The shock comes in where Ezekiel sets it. In a boneyard. In all that the wind and desert heat have left in the aftermath of a killing field's terrible loss of life. Bones. Dry bones.

Now hear the Word of the Lord.

That is, after all, how we sing it. "Dem bones, dem bones, dem dry bones." In the gospel song, the Lord's Word then speaks of connections of one bone to another. In Ezekiel's narrative, the Lord's Word speaks of re-connections, restoring bones to life by the power of God's Spirit.

In the dead and dried-up places of this field, in the dead and dried-up places of your life and mine, another possibility remains. That possibility is the power of God's Spirit to breathe new life into what has been written off as dead and gone. Do you believe that?

I don't mean by that question, do you believe that Ezekiel speaks metaphorically or literally about this field of dry bones. I don't even mean by that question, do you think that Ezekiel or one of his editors wrote these words and placed them in God's mouth. What I mean is: Do you believe that God's Spirit can bring life to you and to creation?

Remember also that "you" in Ezekiel's word is plural, not singular. God does not speak this word to Ezekiel alone. God does not speak this word to each individual's skeletal remains. God speaks this word to "the entire house of Israel" (verse 11). Not once but twice, God declares the "you" in whom Spirit will bring life to be "my people." The vision of Ezekiel 37:14 promises a restored community. It's not

just that God likes you personally and wants you exclusively to have a future. God bestows Spirit to restore life to "you all." To us all.

"I will put my spirit within you, and you shall live." That word offers new hope to your communities and relationships. It offers that word especially to those places that seem dried up and dead, without hope. And it seeks witnesses like you, willing not only to speak that word, but to live by its hope.

What "valley of bones" stands between a community you are part of and hope? How might these words of Ezekiel 37:14 empower you all, together, to open to the Spirit's possibilities of new life?

Sunday
"Come to me, all you who are struggling hard and carrying heavy loads."
Matthew 11:28

In the liturgy of the Evangelical and Reformed Church, the tradition in which I was raised, the invitation to the Lord's Supper always included these words of Jesus. "Come unto me, all ye that labour and are heavy laden, and I will give you rest" (KJV). As a child, I understood the "rest" thing. But only over time have I come to appreciate the significance of Jesus' preceding words. For this invitation seeks out a specific audience for its gift. Those who labor and struggle hard. Those whose backs or spirits are heavy laden and carry heavy loads.

Are you one of those?

Confession is good for the soul. The church has traditionally stressed the importance of confessing sin. And for good reason. Those who see no fault in themselves are generally hard to live with, badly mistaken, or something of both. But the church, on occasion, has overdone the confession-of-sin emphasis to the exclusion of other confessions in need of regular airing. Sometimes the baring of the need for God in life — and what else is confession but being honest to God — is not so much for forgiveness as it is for strength. Or comfort. Or rest. Or the assurance that God has not left the premises.

Listen to the psalms. Their outright confessions of sin are significantly outnumbered by confessions of raw need for God's intervention — and laments that God seems too far or too long removed. "How long . . . O Lord?" (Psalm 13:1). "Why have you forgotten me?" (Psalm 42:9).

Have you heard those cries before? More to the point, have you raised those cries before?

If so, Jesus' words may become clearer in meaning and promise to you. For the ones who lift up such cries are the ones toward whom today's Way Word is aimed. The ones who come to the place in their lives — in your life — where God seems too far or too long removed are

usually brought there by carrying heavy loads or struggling under hard labor. The load of illness or estrangement. The struggle with making ends meet or making sense of what defies sense.

If you have ever found yourself in such a place or time, if you are now in such a place or time, Jesus offers this word to you. To bring rest in the midst of your labors. To bring peace in the midst of your struggles.

What has become a burden and struggle in your life? Envision Christ speaking today's Way Word to you. Open to the rest it offers. Envision this every time the burden or struggle looms before you.

Monday
"Allow the children to come to me." **Luke 18:16**

In the field of education, "performance-based" salary links teacher salary with teacher performance. In business, "performance-based" management sets standards and goals for workers to achieve — or else. "Performance-based" anything operates on a fundamental motive: production. Your value is a function of your production. More cynically, you are only as good as what you produce. So what might performance-based religion look like?

Mothers bring babies to Jesus in Luke 18 so that he might bless them. The disciples, in good performance-based fashion, attempt to send them packing. There is much to be done, you know. Jesus has just gotten through giving some self-righteous adults what for. Entry into Jerusalem looms on the horizon in chapter 19. Serious matters and serious persons await. No time to be bothered by little ones who can't really do anything anyway.

"Allow the children to come to me." This text has sometimes been reduced to sentimentalism verging on the consistency of warm maple syrup. But something more profound than "Jesus likes wee little children" is at work here. This story is not a proof-text for children's times with the pastor, where everyone gets a chuckle out of the cute things that kids say. "Allow the children" is an abrupt statement that rules out performance-based religion from the gospel of Jesus Christ.

The clue for that comes in Luke's prior identification of those whom these mothers bring to Jesus: babies. These are not confirmation-ready youth poised to take on the mantle of faith and engage in service to others. These are not even little ones who might grasp a parable drawn from nature or a simple teaching of love. These are infants. Such ones are entirely dependent on others for food, for nurture, for life. There is nothing "performance-based" about them at all.

Yet for such ones, Jesus makes room. Later in that same verse, Jesus bids you to remember that "God's kingdom belongs to *people* like these children." It is not their innocence or their openness to trust and wonder that qualifies such ones or those like them for the Kingdom. If that were so, *qualifies* would mean God's realm reverts to a matter of merit.

God's kingdom is not merit-based. It is not performance-based. It is grace-based. What you and I hold in common with such infants that Jesus welcomes and blesses is our utter dependence on grace for Christ's welcome and inclusion. God values you for who you are.

Who might need to hear they are welcomed for who they are rather than what they can or cannot do in your community? your church? How might you need to hear and trust that word, *grace*?

Tuesday
"You are fellow citizens, . . . you belong to God's household."
Ephesians 2:19

Where do you belong? That is, where are the places and the relationships where you feel yourself welcomed and valued by others; where you in turn feel yourself free and able to contribute to the life and liveliness of those places and relationships?

If you take today's Way Word seriously, you belong in church. Do not hear that in an accusatory or scolding tone, as a truant officer might reprimand a student skipping class with "you belong in school." Rather, hear "you belong in church" as an invitation offered with a welcome and valuing of who you are extended your way.

Consider the original context of these words. Ephesians 2 sought to reconcile two long-separated groups. The conventional wisdom was that Jews and Gentiles did not belong together and, thus, need not welcome or value one another. Traditions and prejudices on both sides enforced that state of affairs. But into that divide comes the reconciling message of Christ. "Christ is our peace. He made both Jews and Gentiles into one group" (2:14).

In other words, you belong. And be reminded, the *you* in that affirmation is plural. You and I do not belong to Christ as isolated individuals. You and I belong to a reconciled community. The images of "fellow citizens" and "God's household" reveal that sense of community inherent in our belonging.

"Fellow citizens" reminds you and me that the community of faith is grounded in an equality of standing among its members. The old barriers between Jews and Gentiles have been abolished. And in that spirit of peace, Christ continues to break down the new barriers that are asserted from time to time. Progressives versus evangelicals. Straights versus gays. Those who insist on the apostolic succession of bishops versus those

67

who don't. Sides are often taken, and aspersions are often cast, with the claim that Christ is on our side. In Ephesians' truth, Christ is not about side-taking but peace-making.

Do you experience such peace marked by welcome and valuing of self and others in God's household? If not, it is because of human sin and pride. If not, it becomes your call and mine to insist on Christ's welcome and valuing of those who come seeking a place to belong.

Christ's peace comes in the embodiment of this insistent message: "You belong." In the community of Christ, you are welcomed. In the community of Christ, you are valued.

In what ways have you experienced welcome and being valued in and from the church? In what ways might you extend such welcoming and valuing to someone you see in need of belonging?

Wednesday
"Nothing can separate us from God's love in Christ Jesus." Romans 8:38

Nothing?

You might think that Paul has gone a bit overboard here. All manner of things can get in the way of God's love in this world. Greed. Injustice. Torture. Apathy. We could make a very formidable list for what erects barriers in the way of God's love. But give Paul credit. In the verses preceding today's Way Word, Paul compiles such a list. It includes not only experiences (harassment, death) but systems ("principalities and powers," to borrow from the King James Version of this passage) that frequently weigh against God's love. In fact, just in case anyone might think there is an exception, Paul adds at the end of his list: "any other thing."

Nothing can separate you from God's love in Christ Jesus.

Such words look good on paper and sound good in pulpits. But Paul does not write them to impress you with eloquent prose. Paul writes them to companion you in all those times when it might seem, for the life of you (figuratively or literally), they do not hold true.

"Nothing can separate you" offers to be your companion when you stand beside the grave of a loved one—or when your life arrives at that precipice. Such moments can be extraordinarily challenging, for even the best of memories cannot totally heal the loss at hand. Does that one whom you lay to rest—will you at the time of your own death—utterly cease to be beyond the inevitably dwindling reminiscing of friends and family? Or does nothing, *nothing*, separate you from God's love in Christ Jesus?

"Nothing can separate you" also offers to be your companion when all of those experiences that appear to contradict "nothing can separate" solicit you to live as though love is not the final and ultimate word and, thus, not a word or value with which to be greatly bothered when it

WAY
WORDS

comes to your conduct of life now. Why bother to be just, when the world is filled with injustice? Why bother to regard the poor and vulnerable—and why not kowtow to the rich and powerful—when those appear to be the way to get ahead these days?

Why? "Nothing can separate you from God's love." Love, not only as God's age-lasting gracious acceptance of you but love, as God's enduring ethic and vocation for those who so know themselves valued and companioned—and empowered.

God, you offer love's embrace and its call. Remind me that your love in all of its facets will never abandon me and that there is nothing in this world that can separate you from those you love.

Week Five
Faithful Practices

How do you treat Sabbath as holy?

I remember as a child going to the neighborhood Katz Drug Store on Sundays. I recall nothing of what we bought. But what stands out in my mind were large white sheets draping shelves of items that could not be sold on Sunday. Apparently the Missouri "blue laws" (ordinances legislating what businesses could remain open and what items could be sold on Sunday) considered the sale of non-essentials such as cosmetics and toys as breaches of Sabbath.

I also recall a story told by my late father-in-law. He grew up in a small town in Oregon. He was active in the church as a youth, largely because of the ministry of his church's youth pastor. One Sunday afternoon, the youth pastor played in a local baseball game. The next week, the church fired the youth pastor for breaking the Sabbath. My father-in-law decided then and there that he wanted no part of such a community.

How do you treat Sabbath as holy?

The regulations of Deuteronomy that follow today's Way Word emphasize that no work is to be done. "No work" originated the blue laws' attempts to legislate against non-essential work. Looking back, I wonder about the clerks in the Katz Drug Stores. Were they keeping

Sabbath so long as they sold bread or cough syrup, but not lipstick or yo-yos? Looking around now, as the husband of a 9-1-1 telecommunicator who works Sundays, along with the fire and police and ambulance personnel who depend on her dispatching, are they all Sabbath-breakers?

The commandment calls for setting aside one day for Sabbath abstention from what is work to you. But is abstaining from work on Sunday (or Saturday, or whatever day your work schedule allows for a Sabbath) the whole dynamic of how you keep the Sabbath?

Unlike the commandment in Exodus that links Sabbath rest with God's resting on the seventh day of Creation, the commandment in Deuteronomy links Sabbath rest with God's deliverance of Israel from slavery in Egypt.

We do not keep Sabbath by reclining in a hammock or pursuing leisure to the point of exhaustion. Sabbath-keeping remembers God's disruption of life being defined by unrelenting and exhaustive labor. Sabbath-keeping practices a worshipful celebration of who gave you life and freedom. Sabbath-keeping rests and renews in the liberating knowledge that what we produce in life takes second place to whose we are in life.

Plan to spend your Sabbath this week intentionally reflecting on God's deliverance of Israel from Egypt. How might that shape and transform your practices of keeping Sabbath?

Friday
"Let justice roll down like waters, and righteousness like an ever-flowing stream." Amos 5:24

Two very different types of watercourses are found in the Bible lands. Year-round streams may run muddy in the rains and low in the dry spells. But their dependable flow makes them integral to the life that flourishes around them. Wadis are dry most of the year. When rains come, however, they can quickly fill with waters rushing powerfully downstream. They resemble the slot canyons and dry washes of the American Southwest. It is not unusual to find warning signs in entrances to canyons or roadways across washes about not hiking or driving when it rains. The waters roll down irresistibly, sweeping away anything in their way.

Amos proclaims that doing justice is central to faithful practice of covenant. The prophet warns about the judgment entailed when justice goes ignored or is perverted. Affluence constructed on the backs of the vulnerable will come to ruin (4:1-3). Today's Way Word immediately follows a segment that describes how the practices of injustice recounted in 5:10-13 render even worship offensive to God (5:21-23). Covenant and faith rely on the practice of justice.

So recall Amos's imagery of rolling waters and ever-flowing streams. Each set of watercourses depicts qualities of the justice God summons through Amos. Ever-flowing streams provide reliable sources of water necessary for life. Justice does the same for community. Like such streams, the practice of justice needs to be reliable. That is, it needs to always be available to whoever needs its gift. Amos makes clear that a community that does not practice justice in matters of social equity is without hope of life. Social justice and faith are inseparably joined.

Amos also links justice to the waters that "roll down." That is, the course of justice is to be like waters rushing down a wadi, sweeping aside anything in its way. Negatively stated, that is the judgment Amos announces to ancient Israel and any who repeat her folly. Privileges and institutions will be swept away when justice goes ignored or is perverted. Positively stated, the rolling waters of justice reflect the irresistibility of what God deems just and good.

Injustice may seem to hold the upper hand at times, rendering a societal landscape as bereft of justice as a dry wash is of water. But the waters of God's justice will flow: sweeping away what feebly attempts to stand in its way; providing life to those who practice its call.

What is an issue of justice in your immediate community or wider world that you have a passion for? What might you do this day, this week, to practice justice? Commit to doing one of those actions, and let the waters of justice flow through you.

Saturday
"You must love them as yourself, because you were immigrants."
Leviticus 19:34

The community I live in was settled by Finnish immigrants. In our phone book, we don't have a page full of Smiths but we do have one of Wirkkalas. Some years ago, a local writer published a collection of narrative poems about the Finns who settled this area. She entitled it *Remember Where You Started From.*

Remembering where you started from grounds the ethic of today's Way Word. We may be more comfortable with the command to practice love of neighbor that occurs earlier in verse 18. Neighbors are the people we live nearby, whom we know. Neighbors are, by and large, like us.

But immigrants?

Earlier biblical versions softened the scandal of this command by translating the word there as *sojourners. Sojourners* seems pleasant enough, certainly not part of our daily vocabulary. But do not mince words or translations: These folks whom Leviticus enjoins us to love are immigrants. They are people uprooted by crisis or opportunity who turn up in someone else's land. It is not a new story. The reason God links love for immigrants with "because you were immigrants" is because that is how Israel came to be. The twelve tribes, whose names neatly correspond to the names of Joseph's brothers, immigrated to Egypt because of crisis (famine) and opportunity (Joseph has a plum job and can take care of us).

Immigrants sometimes run the danger of being seen apart from you and me because they hold on to traditions and language from their land of origin. I am reminded that my home church in St. Louis did not use English in worship until the outbreak of anti-German sentiment ushered in by World War I. An even more ancient reminder is Israel in Egypt. An entire generation passes for the Israelite immigrants there, and still they retain sufficient distinct identity so as to allow Pharaoh to fear

and then enslave them. The remainder of Exodus narrates whose side God takes when immigrants not only go unloved but oppressed.

Many words and commands swirl today around immigrants. Fences are erected, figuratively and literally. But lest the day be handed over to the tide of fear if not outright hatred, Leviticus adds this stunning word to the conversation. Not only are immigrants to be loved, but to paraphrase the old comic strip *Pogo: We have met the immigrants, and they are us.*

Love the immigrants? Remember where you started from.

How have you experienced being uprooted from what is known and familiar? In what ways might God use those experiences to help you identify with and practice love of immigrants?

Sunday
"Keep on praying." Colossians 4:2

Praying as a practice of faith is obvious enough. Ample biblical texts urge or narrate the practice of prayer. Whatever you conceive prayer to be ("Prayer is the conversation of the heart with God" follows me from the catechism of my youth), prayer belongs at the core of faithful relationship with God.

But what exactly is meant in today's Way Word by "*keep on*" praying? Is it prayer as incessant God-directed chatter? Jesus rules that out in the Sermon on the Mount. "Don't pour out a flood of empty words" (Matthew 6:7). God's knowledge of your needs and those of the world precludes the necessity of your having to ramble on in public or private prayer.

The Greek verb translated here as "keep on" is a compound word. Its main root means "to remain strong, to endure, or to persist." The prefix attached to it emphasizes the element of time associated with such action. It is not short-lived but persevering over time. The verb occurs only ten times in the New Testament, three of those in direct reference to prayer. Romans 12:12*b* repeats Colossians 4:2 almost verbatim: "*devote yourselves to prayer*." The verb also describes the community's perseverance in prayer between Jesus' ascension and Pentecost (Acts 1:14).

This latter episode illustrates prayer that "keeps on." The community lived in the in-between time of Jesus' departure and the Spirit's gift. They could have ceased prayer in grief over the loss of Jesus' immediate presence, waiting for God to make the next move. Their prayers could have incessantly badgered God to put things back the way they used to be. Inertia and nostalgia can interrupt conversation of the heart with God. Inertia and nostalgia can take their toll on faith. But the early Christian community persisted. There was no certainty as to how long this "interim" would last. Yet the community persevered in prayer. They did not give up. They did not kick back. They prayed. They kept on.

You and I live in in-between times as well. You and I live in the moment between the promise of God's reign and its fulfillment. "Keep on praying" calls you to prayer that is not incessant but that is persistent. Such persistence bridges days and times you feel like praying with those you don't. Such persistence perseveres in the conversation of your heart with God about your life and the world around you.

Keep on praying.

Where do you struggle with persistence in prayer? Seek God's help for greater perseverance. Identify a need in your life or community for which you have passion. Pray with persistence.

Monday
"Forgive us . . . just as we also forgive." Matthew 6:12

Has someone ever told you something that was well and good until he or she added a "second thought" that surprised or even offended you? *Can't you leave well enough alone?* is one response offered in such situations. Perhaps you have said it or heard it yourself.

Jesus is teaching the disciples to pray. In Luke's recounting of this teaching, it comes at the request of the disciples themselves. "Lord, teach us to pray" (Luke 11:1).

Be careful what you ask for. You might just get it.

The prayer Jesus teaches begins innocently enough. "Uphold the holiness of your name. Bring in your kingdom. Give us the bread we need for today. Forgive us our sins … (Luke 11:2-4). Now, if only Jesus would have stopped there! We'd have enough to eat. We'd be waiting for God's realm to be ushered in. We'd be forgiven. But no, Jesus can't leave well enough alone. Forgiveness turns out to be a two-way street: *"Forgive us … just as we also forgive those who have wronged us"* (Matthew 6:12). Luke remembers that second clause with an even sharper edge: *"for we also forgive everyone who has wronged us"* (Luke 11:4).

Be careful what you pray for. God might just take you at your word.

Being forgiven is a great thing, especially by God. Weights you could not have carried on your own are loosed from your shoulders and spirit. Guilt that might have nagged you interminably (or terminally!) is cast off. "Forgive us" is the prayer. God's grace is the answer.

But that is not all Jesus teaches about prayer — and with it, about life. Jesus links the practice of trust in a forgiving God with the practice of forgiveness by forgiven disciples. "Forgive us … as we also forgive."

Do you wish that Jesus had not added that second part? There are times that I do. I would sometimes prefer to linger in resentment, in clear celebration of another's wrongdoing. But does indictment or

79

proof of or gloating in their wrong make me a better person? In my more honest moments, not really. As their spellings suggest, the line between vindication and vindictiveness can be treacherously thin.

But there is another way besides holding on to the wrong, to the grudge, to the vengeance. "Forgive us … just as we forgive." Let go. Move on. Accept grace, and be gracious.

Say aloud today's Way Word. Visualize the face of one you find it hard to forgive, and say the Way Word aloud again. As you are able in the trust you are forgiven by God, forgive that other.

Tuesday
"Make disciples of all nations." Matthew 28:19

At first glance, you might think that today's Way Word leaves you off the hook. Unless you are the pastor, unless you are on the evangelism committee or outreach committee, "making disciples" sounds like somebody else's work.

It's not. It's yours. It's mine.

The clue to this comes from what Matthew tells us earlier. The disciples have come to Galilee as Jesus directed. Then comes this curious piece of information. "They worshipped him, but some doubted" (Matthew 28:17). Jesus commissions doubters and non-doubters alike to make disciples. That is intriguing. Jesus draws no distinction in his call between the fully convinced and those who still wonder a bit. So why do we sometimes? That is, why do you and I occasionally think that new recruits—or old hands—need to think or believe exactly as you or I do? That's not the call.

Jesus commissions disciples, doubters and non-doubters alike, to make disciples. Or to put it another way, disciples make disciples. There is an equality inherent in the community so created. Disciples do not make followers of lesser importance—"disciplettes"—to insure that our ways of thinking and doing faith or church are guaranteed. Disciples make followers of Jesus, not followers of you and me or the way we do things here at Old First Church.

Notice too that Jesus does not commission disciples to *go therefore and make church members*. To be sure, that becomes a vital spinoff for Christian community. New blood, which is to say new ways of viewing and doing things, enters the church's arteries. But evangelism is not a synonym for membership recruitment. Making disciples is bringing folks into relationship with God before it is signing them up to teach Sunday school or turn in their pledge card.

The call is to make disciples, and the scope of the call is "of all nations." The church has a disturbing knack for dropping the ball on this one. That is especially apparent when it is noted that the word translated as *nations* more broadly means "any group of people linked by common custom or relationship." The propensity to exclude some people from the fullness of discipleship's call or vocation because of gender or race or any number of biases is indisputable. Jesus' inclusion of doubters and non-doubters at the outset serves as a reminder of the inclusive nature of Christ's call and discipleship's community.

Go and make disciples of all nations. Really, go on!

What does it mean for you to be a disciple of Jesus? How might today's Way Word empower you to share that meaning with someone who is still searching for a way and a One to follow?

Wednesday
"Just as I have loved you, so you also must love."   John 13:34

How does Jesus love you? Your answer to that question is important, because it tends to serve as your magnetic north for the second half of today's Way Word. For you are called to practice love *just as* Jesus loves you. So again, how does Jesus love you?

Grace comes to the forefront. You are loved by Jesus in a way that is gracious. God does not wait until you come to some state of total spiritual enlightenment before deigning to scrape off a morsel of love onto your plate. You are loved by God in Christ in this very moment, as you read these words. To love as Jesus is to love others with graciousness. Such love does not wait for others to measure up or qualify before you extend your love in their direction. You love, whether they are ready or not. For their readiness is not the point. Love is the point.

Goodness also rises to the top. You are loved by Jesus in a way that is not only good, but that is *for* your good. Being loved for your good separates such love from lackadaisical fondness that doesn't really involve itself with what you do or what you make of your life.

An earlier Way Word reflected on the story of Jesus' summons to the rich young man to sell all he had. As noted there, Mark prefaces that hard call with the revelation that those words originated out of Jesus' love for this individual. Loves seeks what is good for another, and good can be painful when it interferes with what is comfortable or self-justifying or even simply maintaining the status quo. Jesus loves you for your good. Thus at times Jesus' love may need to break barriers that insulate you from the greater good of your life. So, too, your love for another's good may result in calls not only hard to hear but to say. When another's good is at stake, whether in crises borne of addiction or bad choices, love seeks what is good, not what ignores the problem.

God in Christ loves you graciously and for your good. Today's Way Word bids you simply yet profoundly to so love others. To love with

grace, unfettered by pre-condition or the guarantee of reciprocity. To love with the aim of seeking the other's good, even at risk of misunderstanding.

Love as you are loved.

God, I do not pretend to fathom the depths of your love for me and for all. Yet, in knowing myself so loved, I hear myself so called: to love. With grace. For the good. In Jesus Christ.

Week Six
Enlarging Vistas

Thursday
"I will also appoint you as light to the nations." Isaiah 49:6

I once was graced to hear the late Tom Hunter sing his song "Coloring Outside the Lines." The title referenced the typical instruction to children, when given already outlined pictures, to color "inside the lines." The song's celebration and encouragement was for creativity that dares to draw colors outside of the lines.

The more I think about it, it is really a gospel song. Why? Because God has this uncanny disposition of coloring outside the lines. One witness to that is today's Way Word.

The earlier verses in Isaiah 49 speak of one called "the servant" in the second of Isaiah's four "songs" about this figure. Verse 5 asserts the servant's task as restoring Jacob to God "so that Israel might return to him." To the Jewish exiles in captivity and those dispersed as the result of Babylon's earlier conquering of the land, this is no small promise. There will be return. God will be on the move—albeit, at this point, for the sake of Jacob and Israel. The words of Isaiah seemingly form the thick stenciled lines in which the servant is to color God's salvation picture.

But even before the hues of joy and homecoming can be neatly filled inside those lines, God's saving colors spill outside their boundaries. In the phrasing of the NRSV, the task of restoring Jacob and

Israel is now said to be "too light a thing" (verse 6) for the servant. "I will give you as a light to the nations." Suddenly, the lines that once circled some out are now expanded to make room for all.

You might have thought that taking care of one's own would be ministry enough for Isaiah's servant. Not so, says God, to the servant.

And not so, says God, to you and me.

To be in the service of this God bids you not to become fixed on boundaries, but opened to grace that abounds in boundary-breaking. That is clear in Isaiah 49. That is equally clear when a lawyer later tries to trap Jesus into setting limits on love by asking "Who is my neighbor?" (Luke 10:29). Jesus' answer by way of the Good Samaritan parable proclaims that ministry, as with neighbor, expands as broadly as God's grace and human need.

"I will appoint you as light to the nations." Where are the lines that God would have you color outside of: in service, in hospitality, in love?

What "lines" did you grow up with in your view of God or neighbor or self that you have since "colored outside of"? What lines might God be leading you to revisit and color past today?

Friday
"I know the plans I have in mind for you." Jeremiah 29:11

I remember my last hospitalization. A fairly routine surgery went well; but the second day after, I developed an internal infection. Several indecisive tests and ineffective antibiotic efforts later, I had trouble seeing any good way forward through the haze of fever and drugs. I was living in the moment, and that moment was anything but good.

At the depth of this, after returning to my room following an MRI, a member of my surgical team strode in. I don't recall his exact words, but they basically went: *I know what is wrong here, I am going to fix it, and you are going to get better.* His voice was not arrogant but confident—and confidence-instilling. Within an hour of what I took to be a surprisingly simple procedure he carried out at my bedside, the fever was gone; I was feeling better; and I was not only seeing a good way forward, but on my way home the next day.

Living "in the moment" can be fine when all is well. But when "the moment" fills with pain or despair, and those are all you see and feel, something needs to change. An assuring word is needed to bring you back. To restore a vision of a bigger picture than the momentary crisis that overwhelms. To reopen the future to life's possibilities.

To Israel in exile, God promises such a word in today's Way Word. "I know the plans I have in mind for you." When things spiral out of control, when your knowledge cannot see a good way forward, God assures that there is more than meets your eye at this moment. God assures that the plan is known and not forgotten. In doing so, God assures that *you* are known and not forgotten. To Israel in exile, God reveals that the plans are not unending captivity and irreversible judgment. "They are plans for peace...to give you a future filled with hope."

Maybe you are not in a crisis moment now, but someday you will be. And in that day and in that moment, you need to know that all does

not reduce to what might seem momentarily overwhelming or all-encompassing. You are known to God. The plans God has are not for your suffering or despair—but for your good. So that you may live with hope. So that you may experience peace. God knows.

Call to mind someone who feels trapped in an overwhelming crisis, whether of relationship or health or spirit. Pray for that person. Do what you are able to assure him or her that he or she is not alone.

Saturday
"I will pour out my spirit upon everyone." **Joel 2:28**

I first started to see the two of them when I walked home from school past the auto body shop where they worked. Today the label that would be laid upon them would be "developmentally disabled." Back then, the terms were much harsher.

I later started to see the two of them in the narthex of my church, handing out bulletins before worship. I didn't know what to make of this. Was this wise? What impression did they have on visitors whose first contact with the congregation would come from these two? What did this say about our church?

I now believe that I know what I should have known then. "I will pour out my spirit upon everyone."

Sometimes, and this is as much personal confession as offered observation, the church wants to put an asterisk on Joel's "everyone." It is fine to read Scripture with *everyone* and *all* figuring prominently. But when it comes to whom we want in our pews or pulpits, when it comes to folks we fall over backward to recruit and those we would be more than happy to have check out the church down the block, the asterisk comes into play.

But Joel, like the Spirit to whom he testifies, deconstructs our attempts to homogenize community into those who look and think in our image. Listen to the characters Joel lists after our Way Word as those upon whom Spirit pours out—and welcomes in. Sons and daughters: the ones about whom conventional wisdom says they should be seen but not heard. Spirit gives them the voice of prophecy. Old men (and women): the ones stereotyped as living in the past as their days draw to a close. Spirit gives them dreams for new days. Male and female slaves: the ones who have no rights and no place outside of subservience. Spirit gives them place and freedom in the new community.

89

God pours out Spirit upon everyone.

You are graced to belong to such a community. And you are called to be gracious as part of such a community. I did not perceive that long ago. Those two men handing out bulletins in the narthex did not need my stamp of approval for whether they measured up to "standards." They already had that approval. God's Spirit saw to that, as did the wise and gracious church leaders who entrusted bulletins and welcome into their care.

Pour out your Spirit upon me, O God, that I might come to see the whole of your people upon whom Spirit is poured besides me and those like me.

Sunday
"Whoever hasn't sinned should throw the first stone."　John 8:7

What do you experience in the guilt of another: a vindication of self? an occasion for scorn? an invitation to take a deeper look into the mirror?

Religious leaders bring a woman to Jesus. She has been caught in adultery. Who did the catching is not clear, and stunningly absent is the man who partnered in this offense with her. It is as if he doesn't matter; and in the purpose of these leaders, that is precisely the point. It is not so much her person as her guilt that interests them in an attempt to test Jesus. The law is clear about her sin and its punishment by stoning. Their question to Jesus of "what do you say" intends to entrap him in one form of guilt or another. *Let her go* breaks Torah. *Go ahead and kill her* could be taken as a failure of compassion. What do you say?

Jesus says, "Whoever hasn't sinned should throw the first stone." Which brings us back to the opening paragraph. The woman so caught undoubtedly provided a convenient assurance of scornful self-righteousness for those leaders. So long as they did not do what she did, they felt that they held the higher moral ground.

Do you ever fall into that trap? Reading the newspaper, watching the television, or surfing the Web can quickly convince you that the world suffers no shortage of folks who do not measure up to your standards of decency. So viewed, it becomes easy to judge them not as persons of value but objects of derision. Or worse. Consider John's narrative. Who this woman is does not matter. Her guilt is simply paraded forward as an object lesson to ensnare Jesus.

But snares can also entrap the ones who set them. "Whoever hasn't sinned" is not a license for the sinless to take aim and fire. It invites those leaders—and you and me—to look in the mirror. In doing so, it brings the challenge of seeing that other as you and I are seen. Not as objects of scorn consigned to God's wrath, but as persons of value sought by God's grace.

Taking solace in the guilt of others does neither them nor you any good. Good comes in seeing your common standing with the whole of humanity and the common grace that would say to you as it said to that woman: "Neither do I condemn you."

When have you felt and acted as the leaders in this narrative? as the woman? What difference will this Way Word make in the way you look at others and the way you see yourself today?

Monday
"When you have done it for one of the least of these, . . ."
Matthew 25:40

I don't know who ingrained the importance of prepositions in me, or when. Most likely it was Miss Enright, my middle school English teacher. She insisted on details of grammar like no one I have ever known before or since. And I am forever in her debt.

For instance, take today's Way Word and its first preposition: *for.* It is such a small word that you might think that it has little significance. But consider how the meaning shifts if doing things *for* the least of these becomes doing things *to* the least. *For* suggests a sense of advocacy, acting on behalf of those identified as "the least." *To* eliminates that sense of advocacy. Those identified as the least become mere objects of actions done *to* them — or to employ another preposition, indifferent actions inflicted *upon* them.

I do not draw that contrast between *for* and *to* the least of these as a mere exercise in grammar. The world operates too often on the basis of what is done *to* the least of these rather than *for* them. Consider the rhetoric by which more than a few prescribe social and financial antidotes to the lingering economic crisis. Do you hear great clamoring over protections for the least from the halls of power or privileged media perches? Or is that difficult to discern over the din of ensuring that we keep inviolate the fortunes and good fortune of those who are anything but the least among us? In my biased perspective, what is being done to the *least of these* in the rush to become sycophants to the *greatest of these* is shameful.

And worse.

To define such action theologically: It is sin of enormous consequence. Why sin? Sin signifies separation from God. In the parable from which today's Way Word arises, separation from God results precisely

from indifference (it need not be outright hostility) to actions done *for* the least. "When you haven't done it for one of the least of these, you haven't done it for me" (Matthew 25:45).

Matthew places this parable and our Way Word during Holy Week immediately before the plot to kill Jesus. It is, thus, by nature a Lenten word, beckoning your discipleship of the One who comes *in* the least among you.

How would you treat Jesus if he were to someday stand before you? Your answer is revealed in what you do *for*—or *to*—the least among you now.

Who comes to mind when you hear "the least of these" in your community? in your church? in your life? Read Matthew 25:31-45. What might you—and what will you—do for those "least" ones?

Tuesday
"God doesn't show partiality." Acts 10:34

The scene is from the movie *The Godfather: Part II*. A former member of the Corleone crime family is to testify at a Senate racketeering hearing. Shortly before the proceedings, Michael Corleone enters the room. He is accompanied by the witness's brother. The witness sees the face of his brother. No words are exchanged. But when it comes time to testify, the witness recants his previous depositions against the Corleone syndicate.

It's all about face.

The Greek verb translated as *show partiality* in Acts 10:34 is a compound word. The prefix means "face." The suffix means "to take or receive." So to *show partiality* connotes being taken with or swayed by faces. In the movie, the face of the witness's brother sways truth-telling into perjury.

In today's Way Word, Peter testifies to God's not being swayed by faces. Peter does so in the wake of visions that he and the Gentile Cornelius saw that brought the two together and, in turn, opened the church to Gentiles. Peter's insight is that God's impartiality rejects taking things or persons at "face value." The face value of Christian community before this episode would have been that Peter is a Jew, Cornelius is a Gentile, and never the twain shall meet. But God, not the church, takes the initiative in opening the community to those previously set apart from it. God is not swayed by appearances or the rigid face of entrenched traditions, even when those traditions claim the stamp of God's approval. God does not show partiality to one group over another when it comes to showing grace, beckoning faith, and fashioning community. God shows no partiality by offering acceptance and love to all.

The nature of God has implications for the nature of God's community. To be gathered by the God who shows no partiality summons disciples to go and do likewise. How good are you, and how good is your church, at not being swayed by "faces"? Plenty of faces vie to sway your judgment. The allure of attracting "your" kind of people—and the fear of allowing those judged as "other" than your norms—can result in Christian community resembling a gated subdivision more than a mixed neighborhood. What "face values" sway you from not only witnessing to God's impartiality, but practicing such impartiality yourself?

Peter proclaimed, "God doesn't show partiality." What do you say? And how will you live what you say?

God, it is so easy to go on face values alone. But you bid me to go deeper in love, with grace, for good. Go with me on that way. In Jesus Christ. Amen.

Wednesday
"To bring all things together in Christ" Ephesians 1:10

Where is this world headed? One expression picked up in my youth seems to fit the judgment of many: "to hell in a handbasket." Such words relegate the future to a shrug of the shoulders and a resigned "What's the use?" A potentially more seductive despair comes in Christian (I use the word loosely) escapism. I do not mean by that the defiant hope of Revelation that utilizes fantastic imagery to debunk earthly powers that claim prerogatives reserved for God. Rather, I mean the translation of faith's hope into a spiritual escape-pod-from-Planet-Earth, where the rapture is less a mystery and more a smug assurance of self-righteousness. After all, have you ever seen a bumper sticker that says "In case of rapture, I'll still be driving"?

All such pessimisms about the world coalesce on the point that everything seems to be falling apart.

But everything is not what it seems.

"This is what God planned for the climax of all times: *to bring all things together in Christ.*" Today's Way Word asserts a far more radical hope than speculation over what happens to freeway traffic on the day of rapture. "To bring all things together in Christ" proclaims the world is not destined to disintegration, but to re-integration within a God-intended unity.

It is a challenge to hold, much less live by, such hope. Disintegration abounds. Children kill children in conflicts around the world, and too often in our own streets. Greed proliferates in the ever-widening gap between rich and poor. The unraveling worsens when the Church retreats from proclaiming much less modeling "the plan" of Ephesians 1:10. Perhaps that retreat owes to our holding the vision as our private secret, rather than the world's gift. Or perhaps, we do not persist in the vision of Christ's bringing all things together because we do not believe it.

But think of this hope's possibilities in the face of such challenges. You and I have God's word that all does not fall apart in the end. You and I have God's assurance that creation's destiny is not in disaster but in reunion.

As a result, God commissions you and me to live in ways that translate that vision of final unity into words and actions and attitudes that bear its witness and live its promised gift here and now. Hope is not your escape from the world; hope is your means to live faithfully within it.

Today's Way Word comes on the eve of betrayal and cross. What hope does this word bring to tomorrow and Friday? What hope does this word bring to your experiences of life's unraveling?

Holy Week

Saving Mysteries

WAY
WORDS

Maundy Thursday
Do This.

"Do this to remember me."   *1 Corinthians 11:24*

Imagine that you are gathered with those closest to you as you near the time of your death. What would you like them to do to remember you by? What might not only call to mind and heart the kind of person you have been, but affirm the purposes for which you have lived?

Jesus faces such an occasion. The night before he dies, he gathers at table with his disciples. The setting is traditionally identified with the Passover meal, a meal itself laced with remembrance. The Passover remembers God's saving activity in deliverance from Egypt. The various foods at Passover's table serve as multiple symbols of that deliverance and its hopes.

With a new Passover at hand, Jesus bids his disciples, then and now, to remember him in a simple meal of bread and wine. Remember me, he says, in bread that has been broken. Remember me, he says, in a cup that has been shared. The broken loaf becomes the sign of the body broken for you. The cup shared becomes the sign of my new covenant.

Eat. Drink. That is how Jesus wants to be remembered.

This is not to say that Jesus does not go remembered, his life's purposes do not go affirmed, in the service you render or the ethics you hold in Christ's example. The insertion of "covenant" into this meal's liturgy insures that ministry and mission are integral to individuals and communities of faith. Discipleship has its tasks. You have your callings.

But for work to be done, spirits as well as bodies need to be fed. So Jesus desires disciples of every age gather at this table. Jesus desires that you gather so that you may be fed.

Perhaps you will gather with others tonight at this table. I hope so. The nearness of betrayal and crucifixion brings an added solemnity to this table's observance on Maundy Thursday. That is the nature of this night. But the fact that Jesus declares his wish to be so remembered on this night of all nights assures that solemnity owes not to resignation but hope.

For brokenness and pouring out are not this meal's dead-end. Paul frames this table's open-end this way. "Every time you eat this bread and drink this cup, you broadcast the death of the Lord *until he comes*" (1 Corinthians 11:26).

Until he comes: eat; drink. So that you may remember. And hope. And serve.

What "feeds" you in the words and symbols of this table? How? If at all possible, gather with others in your church or another church to eat and drink at this table—to remember, to hope.

Good Friday
Remember Me.

"Jesus, remember me when you come into your kingdom."
Luke 23:42

Good Friday services often commemorate Jesus' final words from the cross. I write these words on the same day that I will later lead such a service.

Today's Way Word explores another word spoken from another cross. Except, this word does not come from Jesus. It comes from one hung beside him, whom some traditions name "Dismas." It is not the only word Dismas spoke from his cross. He had rebuked the third one crucified that day for his taunting of Jesus. Dismas had also acknowledged the judgment upon him to be just, while confessing that Jesus had "done nothing wrong" (Luke 23:41). Unlike Pilate, who sought to wash his hands of the responsibility for Jesus' execution; unlike the other thief and the crowd who mocked Jesus from the foot of the cross for his Messianic failure to save himself: Dismas speaks the truth of Jesus' innocence. To this innocent one who hung dying like a common criminal, Dismas asks to be remembered in some kingdom yet to come.

So tell me, is Dismas grasping for straws? Is this a last-ditch effort to connive to get what does not belong to him, which is after all what makes a thief a thief? Or is this something more?

For some, the cross is entirely about human depravity and utter sinfulness. Jesus' crucifixion then becomes the brutal tale of a God so incensed with humanity as to inflict the most excruciating of deaths upon the Only Begotten, so that God's anger at our wretchedness can be placated by innocent blood.

But would such a vengeful God who willingly subjects the one called Beloved and Son have any use, much less love, for a thief?

There is another view to what transpires on the cross and why. This view does not play down the reality or guilt of human sin, or its role in what transpires there. The thief who cries for remembrance confesses that he has put himself in this position. But in place of a ruthless God who demands bloodguilt, the cross reveals the merciful God implicit in Jesus' answer to this thief: "Today you will be with me in paradise." The cross does not manifest the violent imposing of God's wrath at creation on Jesus. The cross reveals the vulnerable embodiment of God's love through Jesus, making known the degree to which that love will go to remember even a thief.

To remember even you.

Jesus, remember me—when I feel forgotten, when I wallow in guilt, when I linger in sin, when I realize that I will not live forever, when I wonder whether love is the final word. Jesus, remember me.

Holy Saturday
Rest on the Sabbath.

"They rested on the Sabbath in keeping with the commandment."
Luke 23:56

Sometimes you can do only so much.

A good gardener knows when it is time to work the soil, enrich it with nutrients, and plant the seed—and when it is time to wait and see whether growth will come. You cannot reach into the soil and pry open the seed to force it to sprout. It doesn't work that way. A good parent knows when it is time to instruct, model, and discipline—and when it is time to wait and see whether growth will come. You can't force a child into maturity. It doesn't work that way.

On Holy Saturday, good women who have readied spices and oils to prepare Jesus' lifeless body for burial cease from carrying out that work. Their inactivity is not borne of despair or laziness or denial. Rather, they know what time it is. It is Sabbath. It is the day set aside to observe that you can do only so much. Work is not the be all and end all of life. Or faith. There is need for rest. There is need for remembrance of the One who delivered Israel from unending labor in Egypt. There is need for remembrance of the One who rested on the seventh day of Creation.

You can do only so much.

Holy Saturday stands as a gracious reminder that all does not rest on our shoulders, even in the midst of death. The Sabbath rest taken by these women becomes a parable of Sabbath's trust in God. For when you and I reach the limits of what we can do—and what we cannot—Sabbath beckons us to step back. To be still. To renew our spirits in the presence of God and with the gift of community. To accept that some things go beyond our powers to manipulate or change. To trust God when we encounter those limits.

The limits on that first Holy Saturday were defined by a stone-sealed tomb. There was nothing the women could do to change that. The body and fate of Jesus were out of their hands.

But keeping Sabbath on Holy Saturday serves as prelude to the truth that, just because matters are out of our hands, does not mean that they are out of God's hands.

So keep the Sabbath rest of Holy Saturday. For you will need energy for the day, and the news, and the discipleship that dawn tomorrow.

Beyond this devotion, set aside a time of rest for today. In that rest, consider something that is out of your hands at the moment. Prayerfully, and hopefully, place it in the hands of God.

Easter Sunday
Go and Tell.

"Go and tell my brothers that I am going into Galilee.
They will see me there." Matthew 28:1-10

You might have thought that, with Easter's arrival, the journey under-
taken in this book would come to an end. To be sure, there are no more
readings beyond this. But the way of discipleship, for which all of the
previous Way Words have offered signposts, is only just beginning.

God's beckoning of Abram and Sarai to go to the land God would
show them sparked the question that opened this book's first reading
on Ash Wednesday: *Where are you going?* Now, in Easter's dawning
light, the question before women who come to the tomb, and all the
rest of us who listen to their report, is: *Where will you be going now?* The
women are told to go to the disciples, the ones whom the gospels reveal
are missing in action when it came to crucifixion, with news that their
fears had been undone. Beyond that, the women are told by the Risen
Christ to deliver this message that would summon another journey:
Go to Galilee. Which is to say, go back to where this story began in
calls extended to fishers and tax collectors, ordinary persons living in
ordinary places and immersed in ordinary relationships. For Easter's
transformation will have to come, if it comes at all, in the midst of life.

But Easter is not a once upon-a-time story whose narrative closes
when the Gospel narrative ends. Easter reaches into these ordinary
lives of yours and mine and asks: *Where will you be going now?* Where

will you be going—and what will you be doing—now that resurrection has revealed this crack in the façade of death? Where will you be going—and what will you be doing—now that discipleship bids you not simply into sanctuaries bedecked with lilies and alleluias, but out into the world where fear still claims the upper hand?

Abram and Sarai began their walk on the way of faith by journeying toward a promise not yet in sight. The women who came to the tomb, and the disciples who heeded their word, took up their walk on the way of faith by returning to Galilee as an Eastered people for whom resurrection was not their story's ending but its beginning.

What of you? Where will Easter lead you in the way of faith and discipleship, with its promises that stretch beyond our horizons?

Christ is risen. If you say it, then live it!

What difference does Easter make in the way you conduct your life? in the way you look at the future? in the way you practice trust in God and love of neighbor?

Notes

Notes

Notes

Notes